A Bear's Tale

THIS EDITION

Editorial Management by Oriel Square
Produced for DK by WonderLab Group LLC
Jennifer Emmett, Erica Green, Kate Hale, *Founders*

Editor Maya Myers; **Photography Editor** Nicole DiMella; **Managing Editor** Rachel Houghton;
Designers Project Design Company; **Researcher** Michelle Harris;
Copy Editor Lori Merritt; **Indexer** Connie Binder; **Proofreader** Susan K. Hom;
Authenticity Reader Dr. Naomi R. Caldwell; **Series Reading Specialist** Dr. Jennifer Albro

First American Edition, 2024
Published in the United States by DK Publishing, a division of Penguin Random House LLC
1745 Broadway, 20th Floor, New York, NY 10019

A catalog record for this book is available from the Library of Congress.
HC ISBN: 978-0-7440-9424-4
PB ISBN: 978-0-7440-9398-8

DK books are available at special discounts when purchased in bulk for sales promotions, premiums, fund-raising,
or educational use. For details, contact:
DK Publishing Special Markets, 1745 Broadway, 20th Floor, New York, NY 10019
SpecialSales@dk.com

Printed and bound in China

The publisher would like to thank the following for their kind permission to reproduce their images: a=above;
c=center; b=below; l=left; r=right; t=top; b/g=background
Alamy Stock Photo: All Canada Photos / Bob Gurr 16-17, All Canada Photos / Dave Blackey 8-9, All Canada Photos /
Stephen J. Krasemann 17bc, Design Pics Inc / Alaska Stock RF / Doug Lindstrand 7br, 20bc, Design Pics Inc / Wave
Royalty Free, Inc. 13br, 23clb, FLPA 20crb, Rolf Hicker Photography 3, Jason O. Watson (USA: Alaska photographs) 8bc,
Westend61 GmbH / Fotofeeling 16bc, 23cla **Bridgeman Images:** Gift Of Elizabeth H. Penn 9bl; **Dreamstime.com:**
David Burke 19br, Antonio Guillem 12-13, 14-15, Klomsky 1, Derrick Neill 7bc, Ovydyborets 19bl, Joe Sohm 9br, Wirestock
11b, Maria Zebroff 18bc; **Getty Images:** Moment / Colleen Gara 4-5, 23cl, Moment / Jared Lloyd 6-7, Photodisc / Don
Grall 10-11, 23bl, Stone / Paul Souders 14bc, 15bl, 15bc, The Image Bank / Mark Newman 13bl, 20-21, Universal Images
Group / Education Images 18-19; **Getty Images / iStock:** Jillian Cooper 22, 23tl, DigitalVision Vectors / mecaleha 4bl,
6bc, llvllagic 10bc; **Shutterstock.com:** EVGENNI 21b, saraporn 17br; **VectorStock:** renreeser 12bc

Cover images: *Front:* **Dreamstime.com:** Anastasiya Aheyeva;
Back: **Dreamstime.com:** Pavel Naumov cb; **Getty Images / iStock:** PCH-Vector cra

All other images © Dorling Kindersley
For more information see: www.dkimages.com

www.dk.com

MIX
Paper | Supporting
responsible forestry
FSC www.fsc.org **FSC™ C018179**

This book was made with Forest
Stewardship Council™ certified
paper – one small step in DK's
commitment to a sustainable future.
Learn more at
www.dk.com/uk/information/sustainability

Pre-level

A Bear's Tale

Alli Brydon

Summer begins.
A grizzly bear walks
on four feet.
The bear walks
in its home.
Its home is
the woods.

grizzly bear

The bear is big.
The bear is strong.

fur

claws

It can stay alive
in the wild.

People honor the bear. They think bears are brave and smart.

art

People make art about bears. They tell stories about them.

woods

People stay away
from the bear.
This is also a way
they honor it.
The grizzly walks
in the woods alone.

mountain

marks

The bear marks a tree.
The marks tell other
bears to stay away.

fight

But if another
bear comes,
the bears fight.
The bear is hurt,
but it stays strong.

The air turns cool in fall.
Soon, it will be winter.
The bear digs a den.

den

It will rest here
for the winter.
First, the bear must
fill its belly.

The bear hunts for fish to eat. People also hunt fish.

The bear picks berries. People also eat berries.

fish

It is winter.
The woods are cold.
There is little food
to eat.
It is time for the bear
to rest.
It goes in its den.

rest

Spring comes.
The bear has cubs!
Now, there are
more bears.
The bears walk
in the forest.
Soon, it will be
summer again.

Glossary

cubs
baby bears

den
a cave or place bears
dig for shelter

grizzly bear
a large kind of bear

marks
indentations left
by something

woods
forest

Quiz

Answer the questions to see what you have learned. Check your answers with an adult.

1. Where do grizzly bears live?

2. How do people honor bears?

3. How can a bear tell other animals to stay away?

4. What are some foods that bears eat?

5. Where does a bear rest during the winter?

1. Woods 2. Through art and stories 3. By marking trees
4. Fish and berries 5. In a den